THE WHITE RIGHT OF HERITAGE

*An Affirmative Action Program
For White Americans*

W. Eurvin Cade

THE WHITE RIGHT OF HERITAGE

W. Eurvin Cade

© Copyright 1998

by W. Eurvin Cade

All rights reserved. No portion of this book may be reproduced mechanically, electronically, or by any other means, including photocopying, without the written permission of the author.

Printed in the United State of America
10 9 8 7 6 5 4 3 2 1 PB

ISBN 0-9662469-0-4
Price per copy: $16.00

If you would like the author to speak at your business, school, or organization or to place an order for *The White Right of Heritage*, please write the following address:

W. Eurvin Cade
Post Office Box 1028
Jacksonville, Arkansas 72078

DEDICATION

This book is dedicated to my parents who planted in me, the seeds of respect for all people, the desire to obtain an education, the need to work harder in order to succeed, and the self assurance that I was somebody. This book is also dedicated to my very special lady, Sheryl, who recently asked me, "When are you going to write the book?"

Humans, individually and collectively, have an inherent need to be better than other humans.

You MUST read this book TWICE.

The book is short, easy to read, and to the point.

The White Right of Heritage is NOT a politically correct book.

This book explains issues that have never been discussed before.

WEC

Contents

Introduction	7
One	9
Once Upon a Time in White America	
Two	12
The White Right of Heritage	
Three	17
Power: The Reason Groups Discriminate	
Four	22
Understanding How Discrimination Affects Opportunity	
Five	30
The Psychology of the White Right of Heritage	
Six	38
Education: The Key to Equality and Power	
Seven	44
Black Folks Have Some Really Serious Problems	
Eight	55
What's It All About?	

Introduction

There are millions of Americans—White, Black, Yellow, Red, Brown and multiple combinations thereof, who truly believe that America is the land of freedom, justice, and equality for all. They believe this because in their minds and hearts they try to live up to the grand standards and ideals by which the rest of the world has come to judge us as a great nation. I happen to believe that America is the greatest country in the world. I love America and I love its people. I love the opportunities and the freedoms that we all enjoy as members of this country. However, some members enjoy these opportunities more than others because of the color of their skin. But as many Americans go about proclaiming that all Americans NOW have the same opportunities and that all Americans are equal, they seem to forget about reality. They seem to forget that as grand as our country is, the reality of life is that we are not exempt from the basic needs and traits of human nature that lead us to form groups that will actively seek control and power over other groups. They forget that groups by the very nature of their existence will discriminate against other groups, simply because of those THINGS that they have in COMMON with each other—those things that caused them to group together in the first place.

The White Right of Heritage does exist in America and it

does provide White Americans with advantages over other groups, especially Black Americans. It is not a written rule or document. However, it is a practice that is understood and accepted as a norm by White Americans. This book explains how the practice came to be and why it is the root of the problems between Black and White Americans. In doing so, it provides answers for how WE can overcome these problems by simply understanding them. When we can truly understand the underlying causes for why the problems exist, we can solve the problems. It is not realistic for the majority group in this country to expect a minority group to believe in an equality of opportunities between the two, when the very nature of human characteristics, this country's history, and present day evidence do not support the legitimacy of that ideology. The book you are about to read, *The White Right of Heritage*, should be required reading for everyone. It provides powerful commentary concerning the problems of race relations in America. If you are looking for a politically correct book, then perhaps you should not read *The White Right of Heritage*.

One

ONCE UPON A TIME IN WHITE AMERICA

Once upon a time, in the land of White America, long before the accursed rule of Affirmative Action was invoked for the minority populations of Negroes, the Others, and Females, Whites received special treatment. These minority groups of Americans were considered to be the unworthy ones. The majority population, known as the Whites or the worthy ones, lived in peace and prosperity with the knowledge that their unwritten rule of "The White Right of Heritage" was the true law of the land. In those days of bliss, it was understood by all that the White folks would receive preferential treatment in all situations where the Negroes, the Others, and Females were involved. But this was as it should be, because this was the legacy given to them by the elders.

The elders were wise, good, and all knowing White men. They knew that God had chosen Whites to oversee the earth because the Bible told them so. They knew that all men were created equal, if they were White. They also knew that the tenets of life, liberty, and the pursuit of happiness were theirs to control, because this land was their land. After all, this land was made available to the Whites by God, who placed the Indians here simply to serve as caretakers of the land, until such time as the Whites were able to come and claim it. Their rights to opportunity, education, jobs, ownership, leadership, privilege, and citizenship became the tools of power and control and a legacy to all who were White. And thus, the White Right of Heritage was born in America.

But alas! It came to past, that during the years of discontent, the nineteen hundred and sixties, it was decreed by the then evil tyrant, King Lyndon B., that Affirmative Action for the Negroes, the Others, and Females must be established. He unwisely reasoned that this action was necessary in order to give the unworthy ones an opportunity to access the rights of America. And so the days of overt White preferential treatment became an unspeakable memory of the past, but a secret reality of the present. The White Right of Heritage, once a symbol of all that was good and decent about America and acknowledged by all as the way things ought to be, was now available to all Americans. This simply was not right nor fair. What good is preferential treatment, if everyone can get it? To insure that the legacy would be passed along to only the worthy ones, the White Americans developed covert methods of power distribution to which only Whites were privy or familiar.

During this period, White Americans had to suffer the injustice of seeing the unworthy ones receive mandated, but limited preferential treatment. They had to witness people who were not White and not worthy, receive treatment that heretofore had been reserved for them as an integral part of their heritage. But then one day, along came the good Prince Ronnie to lead the White Affirmative Action repeal crusades. Under his leadership these crusades eventually revalidated the White Right of Heritage in America. He decreed "Let there be no more Affirmative Action for minorities, because all is equal and fair in America." And the White Americans responded by saying, "Yes, let us repeal this Affirmative Action, as it is unfair to both the worthy and the unworthy." And so it came to pass, that the Whites voted to adopt Proposition 209 and eventually all mandated and written Affirmative Action programs for the unworthy would become a thing of the past. The unwritten law of the land would again be reserved for the worthy, as the White Right of Heritage would once again be the order of the day. All of the White folks, including their Females and even some of the Other folks, those who could pass for White or were considered White, would live happily ever after. As for the African-American folks (formerly known as the Negroes), well, they just don't seem to understand that preferential treatment is not for everyone. But this is as it should be, in the land of White America.

The End.

Two

THE WHITE RIGHT OF HERITAGE

In case you missed the point of the story in chapter one or you did not understand the story at all, White Americans truly feel that they have what I choose to call a White Right of Heritage. What is the White Right of Heritage? It is an Affirmative Action Program for White folks designed to insure that they are afforded preferential treatment in accessing all of the opportunities in this country. It is a discriminatory process by which they are afforded these opportunities based on the color of their skin. It is simply about power, economic, political and legal control or domination of this country and its systems.

This desire for power and control is not unique to White Americans, to any specific society, any specific form of government, to Whites or even to humans. If you study history you will find that the struggle for power between individuals and groups within societies is consistent and natural in order to accommodate basic needs and survival. If you study animal behavior, you will find that the struggle for power domination of one animal over another is again consistent and natural. In order to acquire power and maintain power, you have to develop a basis for that power and tools that will support your power. White Americans accomplish this by providing systemic preferential treatment to themselves over minorities. Then they create negative minority stereotype norms that suggest minorities are inferior. These negative minority stereotype norms are continually reinforced through the use of the systemic preferential treatment. Visually, Whites occupy the better system positions and Blacks occupy the lessor system positions. This gives the impression that minorities must be "less than" Whites because as a group they seem to have difficulty accessing opportunities. The reality of the situation is that Whites access opportunities better, as a group, simply because they receive preferential treatment over Blacks. This preferential treatment is provided to them based on the color of their skin. However, they will purposely deny that this occurs.

Now, back to the White Right of Heritage in America. White Americans will tell you that their ancestors settled this country, developed its form of government, fought for it, and in general are responsible for the existence of what we know is the greatest nation on earth today. They will tell you that their hard work, moral integrity, and exceptional knowledge, skills and abilities are the key ingredients to that greatness. I suggest otherwise. I suggest that the White power structure in America used every minority grouping that it could as a tool to establish the power of this country and in turn to establish power for themselves individually and collectively. Starting with the inception of this country in 1776, each succeeding generation of White Americans has built on the successes and failures of the previous generations, which is as it should be. Each generation passed on the reigns of power to the next, to insure that the controls of power remained constant and in the hands of the White majority. The control of power was seeded in the hands of White American males. You have to remember that these were people who for the most part, came from the undesirable classes of other countries—debtors, indentured servants, adventurers, oppressed religious groups and in general, people seeking freedom and a better way of life in the new land. In most cases they had no heritage or history that they wanted to claim. This was a new beginning for most of them. This was their opportunity to have power. A piece of the rock.

What they were doing is called creating or establishing a heritage or legacy. Now, let's look at how Blacks were introduced to the American way of life. I realize that a great many Black Americans prefer to be called African-Americans. But being that I am Black and not predisposed to being politically correct, I prefer to use the term Black. Thank you. Now back to my point. Blacks were brought to this country *en masse* to provide a source of cheap labor for the southern agricultural industry. End of story. There were no concerns or designs to expose them to freedom or a better way of life or to allow them to pursue a better way of life. They were not allowed to develop a heritage or mentality, other than that of a slave. Families were separated, education was not allowed, and citizenship was not afforded to them. They were treated as pieces of property and considered "less than human" in terms of knowledge, skills, and abilities. White society made them dependent upon Whites for their well being and up keep and they kept Blacks divided and suspicious of each other. And you know, they seem to do a pretty good job of accomplishing those very same things today. It is a tribute to Blacks as a people that they were able to overcome the situation of slavery and its aftermath to the extent that they have.

But again, if you look at history, you will find that none of this is new. These are all methods used by majority groups, conquering groups, and ruling classes to maintain control and power domination over other groups of people. These techniques have been used by so-called civilized societies starting with the direct descendant groupings of Adam and Eve up through the present twentieth century. White America went to great lengths to create and preserve their history and heritage while at the same time destroying and distorting the history of Blacks in this country. Whites went to great lengths to exclude Blacks from citizenship and the privileges that it provided, such as freedom, education, representation, and opportunity. Why? Because they wanted to believe that as humans, Blacks were not deserving of the same rights as Whites. In order to justify their treatment of Blacks as slaves, they had to consider Blacks as less than, inferior, or subhuman. To do otherwise would not support their inhumane treatment of Blacks as a people under the system of slavery or their subsequent exclusion of rights as American citizens after slavery. If Blacks individually were treated as a whole person, then the White treatment of Blacks as slaves would invalidate the American constitution which advocated justice and equality for all. It would also raise serious questions about the White claims of superiority and the virtue of their supposed higher moral values and integrity.

I understand that at this point, you are probably tired of my historical references to facts of history that you already know. But stay with me. I have to serve up history as a background for your understanding of my concept of the White Right of Heritage. Answer these questions for yourself. Is there anything that you have read up to this point that is not true? Is it not true that White Americans, as the sole owners and operators of power within this country, were afforded preferential treatment with respect to opportunities? Jobs, education, ownership, representation, and leadership have been provided to them by the legal systems within this country for over two hundred years, based solely on the color of their skin. Is it not true that Blacks, Asians, and other people of color were not afforded those same opportunities for participation in the power structure of this country for over two hundred years, based solely on the color of their skin?

Therefore, is it not logical to assume that most White Americans, either consciously or subconsciously, feel that they have a priority right to the benefits of this system because their forefathers established this system and gave it to them as their legacy? It would appear that the methods used by their forefathers to obtain and maintain power seem to work. The secret is simply to afford each other preferential treatment in terms of system opportunity and control, while at the same time denying or limiting minority group access. It is now two hundred twenty-one years later and White Americans still enjoy the fruits of preferential treatment based on their majority status and the color of their skin. They forget that OUR forefathers also helped to build this country. But White folks tell us that it is not fair to provide preferential treatment to one group over another, based on color. Could it be that WE don't have the White Right of Heritage in America?

Three

POWER: THE REASON GROUPS DISCRIMINATE

In a democratic society, decisions, directions, policies and issues are decided by a voting process in which the majority votes determine the outcome. Therefore, political power and representation within this type of system are necessary to insure that a group's needs and problems are properly addressed. In a capitalistic society, you have open competition in a free market in which the means of production and distribution are individually or corporately owned. Therefore, economic power is also extremely important to insure that a group's needs and problems are properly addressed. In fact, political and economic power form the basis of all power in America. The group that can control both, controls everything. America is a democratic society that subscribes to capitalism as its economic system.

White Americans control both, which in turn gives them power over everything else that occurs in this country. They set the policies, make the laws, and decide which problems are important to the extent that they affect the majority population. Through control of the political process, they decide who will hold public office, make the laws, enforce the laws, and govern the country. Through control of the economic system, they decide who can have access to money, jobs, education, and financial opportunity.

Why are we having this lecture on social studies? Well, I'm still building my case for the White Right of Heritage concept and doing quite well, I might add. As the founding fathers were all White, they understood the importance of maintaining control and they realized that control could only be maintained if the country's political, economic, and military powers were controlled by a majority who looked and thought like they did. They also realized that while they constituted a majority at that time, there was the possibility that given the nature of immigration and the slavery system, they could one day become the minority. To compensate for this possibility, women, slaves, and other people of color were not allowed to vote or participate in any system process that provided access to the country's political and economic power bases. What they did was create a legacy for each White male that guaranteed he had the opportunity in concert with other White males to ALWAYS control this country. Is this not preferential treatment?

When Affirmative Action was first implemented in this country, what were the primary complaints from White males? They are taking jobs from Whites and how are we going to feed and take care of our families? Unqualified minorities are taking jobs from qualified Whites. There were never any concerns about how Blacks, other people of color, and females were affected by the preferential treatment that Whites received in this country with respect to obtaining jobs, contracts, entrance to schools, and other opportunities. There were never any concerns about how Black families would exist without proper education and good jobs. And this thing about unqualified minorities taking jobs from qualified Whites, that's obviously a joke. Well, isn't it? Unqualified Whites have been taking jobs from qualified Blacks for years and years and years. They do it now. Power and control are the keys of the White Right of Heritage concept. All you have to do is open your eyes and look around. Is it not obvious who has the power in America, who controls the power in America, and who has the White Right of Heritage in America? Please write in your answer _____.

As a footnote, I mentioned the military as a source of White power control. Since I discussed the other elements of control, political and economic, allow me to briefly expand on the military element of power. Blacks and people of color as a rule were not allowed to participate in the military. The reasons are fairly obvious: if you allow them to fight for the country, you give up some of your power because now they also have a vested interest in the country which allows them to create a legacy of their own. If you treat people of color as bad as America treated people of color, you certainly don't want to arm them with weapons or allow them to assume positions of power within your military. I bring this up because I believe that Black service in the military is probably one of the primary reasons that Blacks enjoy many of the rights that they have today. Black service in the military has always been exemplary. Starting with the Revolutionary War through the present, we have served our country with distinction and honor. It's just that for some reason the history books and movies of this country failed to include their contributions. I wonder why?

Another aspect of power that I believe is extremely important when you are trying to understand why people want to control, dominate, and exert their power over others, and why they choose to exclude, segregate, and differentiate between themselves and others, involves what I believe to be an inherent need in humans to want to be "better than someone else." We have a constant need to feel good about ourselves at the expense of others who we perceive to be "less than or not of equal standing." I have discussed this theory with others who say to me, nah! you are wrong, man is inherently good. My study of history and life experiences suggest to me that this is not the case. Maslow's hierarchy of needs theory identifies the basic needs that all humans must have in order to exist and assigns a priority ranking to those needs. I suggest the need to be better than others as an individual, as a group, or both should be added to his hierarchy of needs theory.

I mean, think about it. As individuals, we all adhere to a pecking order of sorts based on a variety of reasons. We all understand or feel that there are others who are smarter, stronger, more important, etc., etc. than we are. Conversely, we also feel that there are those who we are smarter than, stronger than, or more important than. So individually, we find our place in the pecking order and identify those who we feel are beneath us in terms of "less than" status, for whatever reason or reasons. We then gravitate to others who we feel are similar within the pecking order, form alliances, and then attempt to exert our control, power, influence, or status over the group or groups that we feel or believe to be different than us. This alliance allows us to effectively deal with both the "less than" and "better than" groups. It provides a comfort zone that increases our confidence and ironically makes it easier for us to obtain the other elements identified by Maslow's hierarchy of needs for basic human survival and existence. If you are not familiar with Maslow's hierarchy of needs theory, I suggest that you look it up in order to see how it relates to my theory.

The point is that the actions of White Americans to group together, profess themselves to be "better than" Blacks and Others, and their desire to control what they perceive to be THEIR environment is not unique to the interactions that take place within groups or between groups. The same process also goes on within the so-called Black community on a daily basis. The reason Blacks have not been able to exploit the process that I have described to the extent necessary to establish an effective power base within this society is because White folks have purposely kept us divided, confused, and dependent. A method of control that they have effectively used since slavery days.

Four

Understanding How Discrimination Affects Opportunity

Today White folks tell us there is no need for Affirmative Action programs because everyone has equal opportunities and as such, everyone should be able to make it based on their own merit and abilities. A majority of Blacks long for the day when that statement is really true. But most of us know that that day is not here yet. When I hear that statement from White folks, I usually try to ask them a specific question. I would like for you to answer this question and if you are true to yourself, the answer will be obvious.

Here is the question: You are White and the neighborhood that you live in is White; the church, organizations, and groups that you belong to are all White. Your friends are White and you basically live and interact with other Whites. You know a few Blacks, see them on television, on the streets, and you occasionally interact with them on the job or in some politically necessary social settings. And let's say you own a business or you are in a position to hire employees. Let's say you have a job opening that does not require extensive training or a specific degree and you have four people who apply for the position. One applicant is the daughter of one of your best employees, one applicant is a church member's son who has two children and just lost his job through no fault of his own. One applicant is your wife's nephew who is really a good kid, just out of college, and needs a chance. In case you haven't realized by now, all of these applicants are White. The last applicant is a Black that you don't know, who has good references, a degree, and some experience. Which applicant would you hire? If you are White and true to yourself, it probably would not be the Black applicant. It would probably be one of the White applicants. Please write in your answer _____.

Now most Whites that I ask this question start off by saying they would hire the best qualified, which tells me right off that they are either stating the politically correct answer or spreading bull droppings. The only way that the Black in this scenario would get that job is if the company needed to hire a Black to comply with an Affirmative Action plan and they really needed that hire to make their numbers look good. You could substitute a Black employer in this scenario and make it three Blacks and one White and the answer would be reversed—one of the Black applicants would probably get the job. You see, it's a matter of human nature. Until White folks fess up to this reality of human nature, there will never be real trust between the races. Let me correct myself. There is another way the Black could have been hired. If the daughter of the good employee was a lesbian, the church member's son, a little on the slow side and the White employer hated his wife and her nephew, then the Black may have gotten the job. Maybe. Not probably, just maybe.

The problem with the term discrimination as it relates to

race relations is that for over thirty years we've tried to tell people that it's wrong to discriminate. We've tried to sell folks on the idea that they should not discriminate. I suggest that discrimination is a normal, basic, and instinctive human trait. What we have today is a bunch of folks who deny at every turn that they discriminate. We have a world full of politically correct liars. Everybody discriminates regardless of their color, sex, race or whatever. We all have likes and dislikes and we all make choices. Whether you choose to believe it or not, Whites do discriminate against other Whites and Blacks discriminate against other Blacks. If we choose not to be around a particular person or group of people, then we are discriminating, whatever the reason might be. I am not suggesting that it is acceptable to discriminate based on color, race, sex, or whatever. But sometimes it's not about any of those reasons. Sometimes it's simply because you don't like a particular person or persons, period. If there is something about someone that you don't like, it does not matter if they happen to be a blind White Jewish female from Africa, or a stuttering Black Muslim man from North Dakota. The point is that people naturally discriminate on a regular and daily basis, individually and collectively. And for White folks, or any folks for that matter, to say that they don't, won't, and can't, is a bunch of crap. People do it every day and we all know that it is done every day. Can we have a moment of silence please? Thank you.

For White folks the term Reverse Discrimination has become their battle cry in the fight to end Affirmative Action programs for minorities. They say that it is unfair to develop plans that will give one group an unfair advantage over another simply because of their race or sex. Excuse me, but what the hell has been going on for the past three hundred years. Is there one person in this country who can look me in the face and honestly tell me that White folks have not and do not receive preferential treatment over Blacks in jobs, education, opportunities, and just about any other category that you can come up with, on a regular and daily basis? Is it not fairly obvious that they still receive this type of treatment? And is it not true that White folks have actively in overt and covert ways discriminated against Blacks for over three hundred years? Tell me what has happened in the last thirty years that would make a sane and reasonable person believe that these practices no longer exist? Duh!

Recently I had the opportunity to view an ABC 20/20 segment concerning race relations in this country. ABC sent two men to Saint Louis, Missouri—one White and one Black—and followed them with a hidden camera as they attempted to find jobs, apartments, and shopped at some of the city stores. The results were quite interesting. Allow me to share with you what their hidden camera revealed in case you did not see that episode. Both men applied for several jobs at the same places. However, the results of their efforts were quite different. The White was in each case encouraged to apply for the jobs, given applications, and scheduled for interviews. The Black was told that there were no jobs available. Did I forget to mention the fact that after the Black was told that there were no jobs, the White would enter after him and receive an application, and be scheduled for an interview. Edith, please, say it ain't so!

Next, the two men attempted to get an apartment. The Black tried to rent an apartment at several locations and was told that none were available. The White applied at the same locations and in each case was shown an apartment for rental. When the landlords were asked by 20/20 reporters why this happened, each swore that they were not prejudiced and that some of their best friends were Black. One was even caught on camera making this comment to the White applicant when he applied. "This used to be a nice neighborhood until they started moving in." I wonder who *they* are?

The 20/20 camera followed both men as they shopped in some Saint Louis stores and in three instances the White went into a store and received immediate assistance from the clerk on duty in a cordial and friendly manner. The Black, on the other hand, did not receive assistance from the same clerk even after waiting for a long period of time. In shopping for a car, the White was quoted one purchase price for the car and the Black was quoted a much higher purchase price for the same car by the same salesman. OOPS! Please tell me this is a candid camera show.

It would appear to me that if White folks control the power in this country and with that power they are predisposed to provide each other with preferential treatment, and given the nature of ALL people to discriminate, then we need to continue some type of Affirmative Action program for minorities in this country. Let me comment on Affirmative Action. I get so sick of hearing White folks say that Affirmative Action means that unqualified Blacks and minorities are being hired over qualified Whites. First of all, Affirmative Action, as written and in accordance with the law, simply provides qualified minorities—I repeat qualified minorities—with the opportunity to apply and be interviewed. It does not mandate to employers or systems that they must hire or accept unqualified applicants. The only reason many qualified Blacks have the jobs that they have today is because of Affirmative Action. If not for Affirmative Action, many qualified Blacks with college degrees would still be holding janitor jobs. Can we have a round of applause for Affirmative Action? Thank you very much.

In terms of numbers, qualified White applicants will always outnumber qualified Blacks with respect to the number of available jobs and positions. So when we show up for the job interviews, that in many cases have already been filled with a qualified White, we are told oh! that job has been filled. But we do have a janitor position open; why don't you take that so you can get into the system and work your way up. Why must we always have to work our way up if we are qualified from the start? When all applicants for positions meet the objective requirements for a particular position, then subjective factors are used in order to determine who gets the job. For example, will this person fit into the work force, do they have anything in common with the existing work force, is this person likable, etc., etc. This is a normal and acceptable method for selection. However, when the person making the selection is White and the existing work force is all White or majority White, and there is always a large number of qualified White applicants from which to select, as opposed to a few minorities, who will always have a better chance of getting selected? Whites or Blacks? Hello, I can't hear you, what did you say?

Can we agree that Whites constitute the majority population in this country and that Blacks represent a minority grouping. Now let's say a medical school has 20 slots to fill for students and let's say that 50 people apply with qualifying scores ranging from 85 to 95. Now let's say that 40 of those applicants are White and 25 of them have a score of 95. The remaining 10 applicants are Black and three of them have a score of 95. Prior to Affirmative Action the White applicants with qualifying scores were in such large numbers that they took up all of the available slots. Blacks who were qualified with the same score could never enter the school simply because there were no slots available. Consequently, Black applicants could never enter the school because EACH year the process would repeat itself. An Affirmative Action plan would have identified this as a problem and recommended setting a quota of some sort that would have allowed, say, two of the 20 slots to be set aside for qualified Blacks per year to enter the school.

Many Whites would say this created an unfair advantage for the minority. I say, what about the unfair advantage that the Whites had before the Affirmative Action plan. Hello! Is anybody home? The Blacks were qualified but under the White Right of Heritage rule, they could never be admitted because the Whites held an unfair advantage in terms of their numbers. Is it right that Blacks not be accepted to quality schools, simply because the Whites repeatedly take up all of the available slots? Every year? You do not have an infinite number of jobs or resources in a capitalist society. Therefore, if White folks, in terms of their majority numbers and control of the resources, obtain the best of ALL resources that are available, then the only resources that are available to us are those that they don't want. And even then, we have to compete with disadvantaged White folks for those resources.

Since I am talking about Affirmative Action, let me raise another issue that sort of locks my hips. What so-called minority grouping would you say has been the primary beneficiary of Affirmative Action programs in this country? The key words here are, so-called minority. The answer is White females. I personally don't understand why White females were considered to be a disadvantaged class because even though they did not have the White Right of Heritage, they enjoyed all the benefits of this legacy simply because they were the White males mate or rather his significant other. When the White male died, who do you think received all of his holdings, the salvation army? But I guess I can't blame them for wanting to expand the White Right of Heritage legacy to include them. I wonder if they thought of that on their own or if the White males suggested it to them as a way of minimizing the potential gains that Affirmative Action programs could provide to what I call, the truly disadvantaged minority groups. I wonder if there was a conspiracy here. Hey, I'm entitled to believe in the possibility that there was a conspiracy here. Some of you White folks think Elvis is still alive and some of you Black folks think that all Egyptians were Black. All joking aside, the reality of all of this is that again, the White majority figured out a way to maintain control of their power and in effect, to expand and enhance the White Right of Heritage legacy.

Five

THE PSYCHOLOGY OF THE WHITE RIGHT OF HERITAGE

White folks with all of their supposed superior knowledge seem to have problems understanding that ALL Black folks want are the same opportunities and considerations that White folks receive. It's just that simple. When they apply for a job or an opportunity, they want to know that their chances of being selected are as good as a White person's, if they have the same or better knowledge, skills, and abilities. What happens in many cases is that Blacks are told by Whites that they need this and that to be considered for something. Then they find out many of the Whites who occupy the same positions don't have what they were told that they needed. When you continually witness the fact that double standards are being applied to the two groups, you start to distrust anything that White folks say. You start to doubt your own abilities and you become complacent because you feel that regardless of what you do, if you are competing with a White person, in most cases the White will get the job or the opportunity. The problem is you don't have the White Right of Heritage that entitles you to preferential treatment. But my friends, we cannot give up, we cannot allow frustration to beat us, we must continue to compete. No matter how much we think the odds are against us, we have to try. That's the problem for many of us, we give up before we try.

I don't think Whites understand that we resent being talked down to—that we really don't appreciate the little insults that they think are complimentary. For example, when they tell us that there is no need for Affirmative Action because every one has the same opportunities. When they tell us "You are a shining example of how your people should be," or "I can get along with you because you are not like other Blacks." Then there are the statements, that some of my best friends are Black or I have a Black that lives in my neighborhood or one goes to my church, so you see I'm not prejudiced. But perhaps the most insulting statements include, "You know it takes time for change, and if you people would just be patient, things will eventually get better." Or how about this, "I'm not responsible for what my forefathers did to your people. Things are different today, we are all equal." This is one I really like, "You do outstanding work, but you know you have to start at the bottom and pay your dues." At the same time you see others who just happen to be White get available promotions with less time and experience. And you know, I haven't met a White yet who wasn't poor as dirt when they were coming up, even the President. What I don't understand is how most of them appear to be so well-off now and many of them have nothing but a high school diploma. Could it be the White Right of Heritage?

Is it so hard to understand why many Blacks don't trust White folks? I personally don't think it's right to mistrust someone just because of their color, because some of my best friends are White and I have two White families that live in my neighborhood. Have you heard those statements before? I believe that *Generational Conditioning* plays a major role in how Whites and Blacks see each other and in how they interact with each other. Whites as a group, have with each generation always been in power and enjoyed easy access to the many opportunities that this country has to offer through which to better themselves. However Blacks as a group, starting with slavery, have with each generation been either denied access to those opportunities or experienced significant systemic roadblocks and difficulties in accessing those opportunities. Today, White folks would have us to believe that discrimination and preferential treatment on their part exists only in our minds.

A few years ago, I did some work as an EEO consultant for a couple of agencies that were having trouble reaching the goals set out in their Affirmative Action plan for hiring Blacks. Since they were having trouble they wanted to seek relief from the plan. When asked what they were doing to attract Blacks, they indicated that they were going to schools, communities, and mailing job announcements to Black churches and community organizations. With all of these efforts, they were unable to attract qualified Blacks. In fact listening to them describe their efforts made one say hey, you guys are doing all that you can, don't worry about it. But do you know what was uncovered when you dug below the surface of their efforts?

First of all, they could not find Blacks because they were recruiting in communities where there were either no Blacks or very few Blacks. They did not visit communities with a high concentration of Blacks. When they were asked why, their answer was, oh we don't have any contacts in those areas. Now about mailing the job notices to Black churches, etc. A closer look at how this was accomplished revealed why this effort also yielded negative results. Each job notice had a closing date, say January 15th. It was discovered that the notices were mailed out on the 13th of January. Need I explain what was going on? These activities were obviously premeditated and designed to insure that Blacks could not compete at the same level as Whites. Would you say that the Blacks were discriminated against and that the Whites were afforded preferential treatment?

It is logical that White folks would believe and say that everybody has a chance, because they do and it has always been available to them. If they have experienced this advantage for over three hundred years, how else are they supposed to think and what else can they expect? They tend to think on a positive level. Blacks on the other hand, tend to think mostly on a negative level with respect to the system because their experiences within the system have been mostly negative. It is because of *Generational Conditioning*, both consciously and subconsciously, that White folks have certain negative opinions about Blacks and vice-versa. I won't labor on those opinions because we all know what most of them are. But even when we know better, certain events, situations, or conditions can trigger the negative mental references that are the products of our respective *Generational Conditioning*. Phew! Thank God, I'm not a social scientist, I would hate to have to talk like that all of the time.

Now I know that a lot of you, especially you Rush Limbaugh wagon riders, are saying, hey buddy, today Blacks have the SAME opportunities that Whites have. I would say to you, yes we do have many more opportunities available to us today, but excuse me, not the SAME. We have more opportunities today because of systemic changes such as slavery repeal, citizenship, and the right to vote. And it was only after a lot of blood was shed that we got those. However, the ONLY way we could access SOME of the privileges that came with those changes, was through the enactment and enforcement of civil rights legislation, laws, and Affirmative Action. Without those tools, we would still be hearing White folks tell us to just be patient and one day when the timing is right, things will get better.

My dad started off as a sharecropper way out in the country with a third grade education. He and mom decided to move to the city in the mid forties where he got a job as a janitor for a large truck and farm machinery company. He worked for that company for over forty years and when he retired in the late eighties, he was still a janitor. Did I mention the fact that he developed his reading, writing, and mechanical skills to the point that the company had him working to repair trucks and that he also worked the parts desk and handled customers on a regular basis. But he was still paid as a janitor and held that title and pay until he retired. So much for working hard, being patient, and one day things will get better.

I made mention to Rush Limbaugh and I referred to his listeners as wagon riders. Those of you who are ditto heads, please don't take that as a put down because it's not. I happen to listen to him myself, a lot. I think he is a great entertainer and that he has a great show. But I think that a great many of you take him way too serious and don't understand that his primary concern is to maintain and expand his audience—that's how he makes his money. In order to do that, he comes on each day, pushes some conservative topic buttons, tells you how he feels or in some cases what he thinks you want to hear and then sits back for your responses for the purpose of engaging you with his rhetorical banter. The man has fun and it's obvious to me that he enjoys what he does. He tells YOU not to deal with your feelings or emotions when discussing issues, but rather concern yourself with the facts. He tells you that Black is Black, White is White and that there are no gray areas when it comes to any situation involving a liberal or liberalism. However, when the situation involves a conservative or conservatism, there are Black areas, White areas, and a whole bunch of gray areas. You probably don't understand or want to understand what I am saying. But the point is, he purposely makes statements and comments about issues and gives you parodies that he knows will jump start your emotions and feelings. You will want to call him because he stands for what you stand for. He makes the statements that you either won't make or can't make. You are one with Russ, you have things in common. You must get on his wagon.

For example, in one of his shows the issue of Affirmative Action was being discussed and he used an example to illustrate why we should do away with these programs. He cited a story involving a Black doctor who through personal neglect and misdiagnosis caused the death of one of his patients. He indicated that there had been a series of complaints on this doctor concerning his care and treatment of patients. Finally he indicated that the doctor had been accepted in medical school as a result of Affirmative Action over Whites, who in his words were more qualified. Rush used this story as an example of why we need to get rid of Affirmative Action. He pushed a button using that story. However, he failed to mention the number of so-called better qualified White doctors in America who have been charged with the same offenses. He also failed to mention the many Black doctors who as a result of Affirmative Action were making significant contributions in the medical field. But then the Limbaugh wagon riders chimed in with their own little horror stories about Affirmative Action and the argument was won. We don't need Affirmative Action in America. You can always find "a story" to back up your position whether it is pro or con for Affirmative Action. But what good is one story or even several stories? The facts are that a significant number of people who happen to be White, have and do receive preferential treatment over another group who happen to be Black. And, that Affirmative Action has proved to be the only way to insure that Blacks, as a group, will receive opportunities to compete within this system. The White majority will not of their own volition provide Blacks as a group with those opportunities.

The same process is at work in all of the Affirmative Action debates. Many Whites push buttons that are common to them with respect to this issue, embellishing their arguments with nice sounding principles and invoking feelings that will stimulate White anger and fear based on no facts and nothing more than perceptions. Blacks, on the other hand, push their buttons in this argument with facts and feelings that are based on the cold realities of real life, negative system experiences that are easily supported through visual observations, and statistical accounting. In short, White folks say that they BELIEVE Affirmative Action gives preferential treatment to Blacks and that it takes jobs from

Whites. Black folks say that without Affirmative Action, they KNOW that White folks, as a group, will in most cases receive preferential treatment over Blacks. We KNOW that as a group we will in most cases not even get an opportunity to be considered. History will support our contention that this will occur. I wish that I had thought of that shorter statement before I went into all of that Russ Limbaugh spill. Well, it's too late now. I'm not going to let all of that work go for nothing.

Historically, Whites have not wanted to provide power exposure or leadership roles to Blacks. NOW you want us to believe that if we would just do away with Affirmative Action, everything would operate in an ethical and morally legal manner. Excuse me, but nowadays it appears to me that a great many people in power positions are going to jail or being exposed for ethical and moral violations of the law. This would suggest to a thinking person that the country's climate must be amenable towards this type of behavior. But you see, that's the type of oxymoron statements that Blacks get from Whites, which leads them to believe that Whites are talking down to them. I suspect that one of the conditions for gaining the White Right of Heritage is, that you must never admit to other groups that you have this advantage, because after all, they can't prove that it exists. It's not written down, anywhere.

Six

EDUCATION: THE KEY TO EQUALITY AND POWER

Now, let's take a look at how education is used to strengthen and legitimize the White Right of Heritage legacy. Oh! In case you haven't noticed, I've dropped the Other and Female categories from my discussion. Partially because it got tiresome writing it and secondly, while the White Right of Heritage does negatively impact other racial and ethnic categories, I prefer to make this a Black and White issue. I know the Indians are still catching hell, the Southeast Asians are doing okay, and those poor White folks in the Appalachian mountains, well if someone would just tell them that they are White, they could claim their White Right of Heritage, too. Now the Hispanics? Hey you know, they may be onto something, because it appears that their plan of attack on the White Right of Heritage legacy is simply to become the majority population in this country and take over everything. I just thought about that. That might work. On second thought, Nah! It'll never happen. White folks are way too smart for that one. My bag!

Back to education. Education is the key to obtaining power

and maintaining it. This is only if you don't have to actually fight for power, in which case, the key would be to win the fight first. After that, education would be the key. White folks understood this, so they went to great lengths through the use of systemic measures to either deny, totally exclude, or limit participation by minorities in this country's educational system. Again, history supports these types of measures, if your intent is to maintain control over minority groups and insure that you have a competitive edge over them. You keep them ignorant and dependent upon you for the knowledge that they need in order to operate and survive within the system. Secondly, you limit their ability to compete with you for opportunities that are available within the system. You, in effect, maintain your control and power over the system. Smells like the White Right of Heritage to me.

But as it is with all so-called good things, eventually they come to an end. White women started going to school and became the front line teachers for schools under the watchful eyes of a male principal and so one group broke down a part of the systemic barrier. Blacks were freed from slavery and wanted some type of education and so the final barrier was overcome, or so we thought. But not to worry, the White Right of Heritage kicked in. White folks realized that if they allowed Blacks to attend schools with them, the myth they had created that Whites were superior to Blacks would fall apart. It would seriously undermine their control and power domination of Blacks, not to mention the irreparable damage it would do to Billy Bob's and Miss Lucy's psyche when they discovered that there were actually Blacks who were as smart or smarter than they were. The Blacks would find out that they had the same aptitude for leadership, jobs, and positions as Whites and my god, this would be disastrous. Blacks would be able to understand the system, compete with Whites for jobs and opportunities, and eventually obtain a piece of the power and create a legacy of their own. The White Right of Heritage would be seriously compromised. Not to worry. Boys and girls, can you say, Separate but Equal?

The Separate but Equal Doctrine was designed in part to address the (I like this phrase) "Negro educational desires," and you will notice I did not say needs, while at the same time limiting their abilities by making their schooling substandard to that provided by the White schools. I'm certain that the Black leadership at that time supported this doctrine, as it did provide us with something. And after all, something is better than nothing. Hey, that is really a profound statement. It was also a way of preventing the races from mixing and keeping the myth of White superiority alive. And again, they had to protect Billy Bob's and Miss Lucy's psyche and, of course, maintain the White Right of Heritage legacy. The threat that educating Blacks posed to the White Right of Heritage was so great that in the 1920s Whites contributed millions of dollars to Marcus Garvey's back to Africa movement for Blacks. Since slavery was abolished and machines were developed to better work the fields, was there really a need to have them around? Shoot, Homer, let's send 'em back, a lot of them want to go back anyway and it is our Christian duty to help our brethren. Thank God most of us wanted to stay, cause I like it here.

In the 1960s, integration started to become a reality. Today, there are ongoing arguments among Blacks and others over the positive and negative impact that integration has had on Blacks.

Some say we should have maintained the Separate but Equal policy and improved on it by making it truly equal. Others say integration was the only way to go; look at what we have accomplished. This is the one situation that White folks point to when they indicate that we all have the same opportunity. On the surface one would have to agree with that statement. But indulge me if you will. There are major problems in our school system today and much of it involves many of our Black youth. A disproportionate number of our youth are placed in special education programs with supposed learning and behavioral problems. A disproportionate number of them are the recipients of school discipline measures. And many of our Black youth either simply drop out of school or they are passed through the system unable to read or write.

What's wrong with this picture? I attended all Black schools through the twelfth grade and even with the outdated and secondhand books that we had to use from the White schools, we still did a pretty good job of learning. I don't remember there being an abnormal number of discipline problems, students with learning problems, or students dropping out of school during that time, other than the fact that I was always in trouble for doing something mischievous. So what were the differences? I suspect that when integration was forced on the White school system they were not prepared for it, nor did they want it. Secondly, during the 60s and even today what particular group constitutes the largest percentage of our teacher work force? Give up or is it obvious where I am going with this? White women. Now, what group are we having the most problems with in the public school system? Black males. Last question. Since the early

70s what group has increased their level of academic achievement in terms of acquiring a higher level of education? Black females. I'm not going to provide you with any statistics; if you want the proof, look it up for yourself. Besides, statistics are boring to write and even more boring to read.

What I am suggesting to you is this. White females cannot deal with Black males. I believe they have an unnatural fear of them and that their *Generational Conditioning* kicks in when they have to contend with them. I believe that the White female teachers could better relate to the Black females and as such, when they figured out integration was here to stay, they began to truly practice their profession and spend more time and give more attention to the Black female educational needs. I also believe that in the early days of integration we were not ready for it and to some degree we resisted. When our children were disciplined by the White teachers we immediately ran down and raised a bunch of hell because we knew that our children were being inappropriately chastised by the White teachers. And sometimes it was probably true, however, it became a regular practice and we are seeing the results of our overreaction in our children today. The school system's hands are somewhat tied today with respect to administering discipline and so they have decided that the best ways to handle these problems are to put them in remedial classes or just let them go through school dumber than dirt. If I had attended White schools at the elementary and high school levels, I probably would have been put on prozac or some other medication or labeled as a trouble maker. I probably would not have been allowed or able to participate in school activities to the extent that I did within the Black schools. I don't believe that I would have been allowed or able to realize my full potential.

When I attended the Black schools, Black parents knew the teachers and trusted them to teach and discipline their children. When I did something bad at school, I was disciplined there and also when I got home. When I did the little mischievous things that young boys do, I was not branded with the label of having a learning disorder. I was punished and then reminded that I had been taught better than that. We were all encouraged to learn and develop. We were constantly reminded that the only way to be successful, the only way to overcome discrimination, and the only way to compete with White folks, was to get an education. We were taught that you had to work harder than White folks in order to compete with them. Not because we were "less than," but because they understood discrimination and they understood the White Right of Heritage.

You know what the difference was then, as opposed to now? The Black teachers cared for us, first as a person and then as a student. But this attention, concern, understanding, nourishment, and encouragement did not follow us into the White schools. White teachers as a group did not and could not relate to Black children in the same way that they did with White children. Their *Generational Conditioning* would not allow them to get pass the fact that these kids were Black. I may be wrong but I really don't believe that many of them can or do now. Please understand that I am aware that there are other problems that contribute significantly to the problems that our Black youth are experiencing in today's public school system. What I have tried to identify in this chapter are the reasons for the start of those problems and why they continue to get worse.

Seven

BLACK FOLKS HAVE SOME REALLY SERIOUS PROBLEMS

One of the main arguments presented by White folks as to why Affirmative Action should be discontinued, especially for Black folks, involves a comparison of how successful other minority groups have been with respect to taking advantage of the opportunities that are available in America. Aside from the situations that I have presented in the previous chapters concerning how Blacks have been negatively affected by the White Right of Heritage legacy, there is some validity to their argument. But, let's take a look at the comparisons. White ethnic groups should be discounted because after all they are still privy to the White Right of Heritage. But in any event this is what they did. Each of them came to America, established communities in which they were the majority population as a base of operation, and then set about preparing themselves to take advantage of opportunities. So in essence, they came, they established their own communities, they entered the education system, and THEN they were able to take advantage of available opportunities. The

Chinese, Southeast Asians, Hispanics, Filipinos, Japanese, Germans, Italians, Jews, Koreans and any other group that you can name, ALL did it the same way. Many of them still have their initial bases or communities to this day.

What is it in this scenario that is consistent with all of them. First, they established their communities; second, they used the education system to prepare themselves; and third, they took advantage of opportunities and established their own power bases and legacy. Let me put it another way, they employed the tenets of self segregation and partial assimilation until they established a power base and then they became more integrated into this society. This allowed them to maintain their culture, customs, and traditions—their heritage and in short, their personal identities.

Now let's take a look at Black folks. They were brought here as slaves, not allowed to continue their customs and traditions, family units were separated, education was denied and in short they had no identity. But you say hey, that was a long, long time ago. Okay, granted. But stay with me. When we were able to finally participate in this society after the Civil War, we started about to do the same things. We started our own communities, we began to educate ourselves, and we started to build our own legacy, our own identities. And even with the adverse treatment of second-class citizenship, we were slowly building our legacy. But something happened that turned all of that around in the 1960s. That's right, integration. Integration had some extremely negative effects on our process of legacy building.

I believe that during the period of slavery when we had no identity, we assumed the identity of White folks. Because, after all, we took care of them when we were slaves and deep down inside we knew that they were no better and no different than we were. Faced with the dilemma of having no identity, we assumed theirs as a part of our *Generational Conditioning*. When integration came along we eagerly jumped on the bandwagon and went about trying to fully assimilate within this society. The only problem with our attempt to fully assimilate within this society was that it occurred only in OUR minds. It is fairly obvious that White folks did not recognize or acknowledge our attempts at full or complete assimilation. Do you know what I mean by assimilation? Let me define: to make similar; cause to assume, a resemblance; to absorb into a prevailing culture.

With integration, I believe we thought that all of our problems of second-class citizenship were over. So it was no longer necessary to build our own legacy, we would just claim our rightful piece of their heritage and legacy. Big mistake. We lost control of our communities, our families, our children, the beginnings of our power base and most of all, the Black Right of Heritage that our forefathers had worked so hard to establish. We lost our competitive edge of working harder and the foresight to instill that trait in our children. We lost the ability to recognize what was needed in order to succeed in this society, because NOW we had the same rights as Whites. We truly believed that we would have access to all that was good and great about this country. We attempted to fully assimilate within this society because we wanted to be White and we thought that we were White. Player, player! Why did you go there?

I suppose you think that I am against integration. Well, I'm not. I'm simply explaining what has happened to Blacks in comparison to other minority groups who made and are making successful transitions in this country. We don't need to be segregated, we just need to be able to identify the negative effects of integration and take the necessary steps to deal with those effects. I believe that Blacks as a group would have been more successful if they had adopted the concept of partial assimilation as their method of embracing integration as opposed to full assimilation. I suppose you also think that I am saying Black folks have not been successful. We have. However, collectively we have not established a power base that will afford us the same Right of Heritage that White folks and others have established, and we need a power base if we want to be self supporting. I believe that as a group we are too dependent on White folks to solve our problems. I believe that this is just another negative product of integration.

In the late seventies and early eighties, two events occurred that caused a serious problem between Black males and Black females. First was the Equal Rights Amendment (ERA) movement. White females started this movement and reached out to Black females and told them that they needed to join this movement in order to obtain their equal rights to jobs and opportunities. Black females eagerly embraced this movement and joined their White sisters in condemning males, like Black males were really responsible for the dilemma of females in this country. When the smoke died down, the White females received what they wanted and the Black females, well they were still on the bottom of the opportunities list. However they did manage to come up one notch and push the Black male to the bottom of the list. This created a serious split between the two. The next event is somewhat tied to the first, in that with all of the attention to the plight of females in this country, the White establishment found out that they could hire a Black female and fill two squares with one hire action (a minority and a female) In doing this, they increased their compliance numbers by counting them twice. This made their Affirmative Action compliance reports look better than they really were.

The end result, females began to receive priority consideration in all Affirmative Action hiring. With their new hiring status, Black females started projecting some of their White sister's attitudes toward Black males—the attitude that they did not need a man and they could make it on their own. Big mistake. For us as a group to make it in this country or anywhere else, we need to work together. The recipe for a family unit calls for equal parts of a man and woman. Black women are not necessarily the backbone of our community and Black males are not necessarily the leaders of our community. But working together, we form a basis for the development of both. We need to love each other, be there for each other, raise our children together, and present a united front to the White community and the problems that have beset us as a minority grouping in this country. I believe, as a group, we are still trying to recover from this particular negative product of integration. It seems to be reflected in the problems that we are having with our children today.

Black folks need to stop marching around, making a show and complaining about what White folks won't do for us. We want jobs and opportunities, yet we drop out of school, litter, and tear up our so-called communities and then tell White folks they've got to help us. I say so-called communities because there are very few, what I call Black communities, in existence today. Marching and coming up with catchy slogans such as Days of Atonement and Reconciliation will not solve our problems. They only serve to project some self-serving wantabe leader into the limelight as a representative of our interests. Rolling up our sleeves and doing the hard work of raising our children, keeping our families together, getting an education, learning how this system operates, and networking with each other to create working coalitions that will produce strong economic and political power bases is what we need.

I personally believe Black self-help is the answer to our problems as a group, and that the Black church would be a perfect instrument through which to create and operate self-help programs and opportunities. Back in the sixties, the Black Muslims under Elijah Mohammed preached and advocated self-help as a way to equality. The Black church was once a uniting force for our community efforts and actions and we were greatly involved with self-help activities. Today, it would appear by the large number of Black churches, that the churches are too busy supporting the large population of Black ministers that we produce each year to be of any use in addressing community needs. We have churches on damn near every corner. Why don't we get smart and combine some of these churches and memberships to develop the power that will allow us to really accomplish some much needed Black self-help community action. Right now we have a bunch of little kingdoms out there that do nothing but spend their time and energies in the preservation of their individual little kingdoms and the workings of their particular mundane religious ideologies, traditions, and personal self-serving activities. Religion has a higher calling than that and I wish our churches would answer the call.

About power—we had a great deal of political power when we exercised our right to vote, and in reality we still have it, but now very few us of vote. The sad part is that we will vote in national elections for some good looking, sweet talking White guy, but we won't vote in local elections that determine such things as city and county representation, taxation, or other local issues that impact our lives on a daily basis. We have lost our understanding of what it means to vote and how important our vote can be. Whether you know it or not, Blacks have a great deal of economic power. We have the numbers in terms of people and we have a national purchasing power that has been validated. Hey! Check it out. The stats will support my claim. Black folks spend a LOT of money and I call that economic power. If we could only figure out how to marry our political power with our economic power and allow the two to work in unison, we would be on our way to establishing our own Black Right of Heritage.

Education is the key to power and opportunity. We cannot continue to allow our children to drop out of school or to just get through. They must learn and they must be able to compete. We cannot continue to let our children not participate in the learning experience simply because they feel like some White teacher offended them. There is more at stake here than the pettiness of some White person hurting their feelings. Without an education, a whole bunch of people are going to hurt their feelings for the rest of their lives. Without an education it is easy to see why many of our youth involve themselves in criminal behavior. It is almost impossible to get a janitor's job today without an education. If Black parents and grandparents would make their children take responsibility for their actions instead of always bailing them out, I believe that we would see a significant change in a lot of their negative behavior and criminal involvement. Too many times we bail our children out of self-created DUMB problems over and over and over. What's the point?

Before I forget it, let me comment on our continuing struggle to include the teaching of Black history in our public school system. We already know that the system purposely excluded us from history books to imply that we contributed nothing as a people in Africa and that we contributed nothing as members of this country. If you have been following me in this book, then you also know why they wanted to exclude or minimize our contributions. Remember it's all about power, control, and being "better than." I say, if the education system won't include Black history within its curriculum to the degree that we want it to, no problem. We'll teach it at home, in our churches, and in our community programs. It's OUR history and we have access to the technology that will allow us to keep our history alive, current, and available for ALL to see.

And what about Black on Black crime? White folks are not killing, raping, or robbing us; we are doing these things to ourselves and then saying that White folks are responsible for making us do these things. We stand on the street corners and sell drugs and when the police arrest us, we claim they are picking on us. In many cases, this is a bunch of crap and we know it. But it is a lot easier to blame White folks for our problems. If not for them we might have to stand up and take responsibility for our own actions and destiny. We talk about White folks moving to get away from us. Well, if a number of us are robbing, raping, and killing each other, doesn't it make sense that other people might not want to live around a number of us? Do you want to live where your life and property are in constant danger? I don't understand. These gangs and thugs conduct drive-by shootings, kill other Blacks, burglarize Black homes, but they won't go into White areas and do this? Why, because they know that White folks will not tolerate that crap and the judicial system will give them stiffer sentences for Black on White criminal activity. Or rather there is a perception that they will receive stiffer sentences for this type of criminal activity. I think they are probably right.

To all of you young brothers and to you "square heads," (older brothers who should know better) who persist in spending your time hanging with the homies cause of "da love"—that's a bunch of crap. Do something positive with your lives, it's not hopeless until YOU give up. I know. I have been there. A few years ago when I thought that I was on top of the world, some events occurred that caused my world to come crashing down around me. For two years I couldn't find work that I thought was at my level or that paid what I thought I was worth, so I hung out with the homies and dealt with "da love." It damn near destroyed me because with all of the rejection that I received from the system in trying to get back on my feet, I began to embrace "da love" and started to convince myself that this was to be my destiny. Hanging with the homies. That's when reality set in and I told myself there is something better. I put aside my ego and got a $3.25 an hour job—minimum wage—and I've never looked back. Why? Because instead of hanging with the homies everyday, dealing with "da love," I started to occupy my time with positive activities such as working, spending more time with my family, and doing things to better MYSELF. These activities replaced my daily diet of negative love which consisted of drinking too much, hanging around too much, and doing too much of nothing but making excuses for why, I could not make it. If you hang around people who are doing nothing but hanging and banging, then that's what you will do. Hang around people who are working or trying to better their lives in positive ways, and believe me, it will rub off on you. That's where real love hangs out. Why keep giving your money to lawyers, judges, and to the system? It's a game that they are playing with you. Believe me, you are not playing them. You think that you are playing the system? It should be fairly obvious to the average idiot, who's getting played. Tag! You're it Boo.

Finally, I must say something about Black on Black discrimination. I believe we discriminate against each other probably as much, if not more, than White folks discriminate against us. Why, because we won't talk to each other enough about the right things. We socialize and make superficial gestures at being cordial with one another, but we don't talk to resolve issues. We complain about the problems, but we are not willing to work together to resolve them. In most cases, it's simply because we don't like or can't stand the individual or group. White folks work together to attain a common goal and then go on about their business until the next problem. We on the other hand cannot work with someone towards a common goal, if for some reason we don't like them. And most of the time it has nothing to do with what the person or persons have done, it's because of what we perceive they did or did not do. But let somebody mention a march and we're all for that, because we can participate for a minute and then go back home and look at television or tell everybody about the joys and excitement of participating in an historic march. Many of us are reluctant to participate in something that we feel will require too much work or personal involvement. I hope my Black readers don't get offended at my comments because I know that there are a lot of dedicated Black people out there who are committed to positive change and who try everyday to make a difference. But those of you who are doing this, you know who you are and what I am talking about. Don't you?

Eight

What's It All About?

This book is about the White Right of Heritage and how it is used as an Affirmative Action program for White Americans. Whether you chose to believe me or not is irrelevant—the proof is out there for all to see. I believe it is obvious that we need some type of Affirmative Action for minorities. Today there are a great many White folks demanding an end to Affirmative Action programs for minorities in this country. They have even enlisted the aid of some successful and, I believe in some cases, well-meaning Blacks. Their intent is good because as a people we should all want to make it based on our own merit and ability. They advance the charge that Affirmative Action is detrimental to both Blacks and Whites, but they don't provide anything other than rhetoric as a replacement. They throw around statements such as, all you have to do is work hard, everyone has the same opportunity, and everything is equal and so we don't need to give people advantages over others based on race. In a perfect world I would agree, but this is not a perfect world or a perfect society. I believe that Blacks have proven that they can compete on their ability and merit, however, I don't believe that Whites have proven that they, as a group, are colorblind.

Do you remember Clarence Thomas? A few years ago he indicated that Black Americans no longer needed Affirmative Action, as he held himself up as an example of how Blacks could make it in this society based on their own abilities and merit with his appointment to the U.S. Supreme Court. Talk about a bunch of crap. If he didn't know that his selection to the Supreme Court was a Republican party ploy to sway Black folks to the Republican Party, how in the hell can he make quality or meaningful decisions as a member of the U.S. Supreme Court where the ability to logically assess and interpret the law is of paramount importance? Talk about an ox .. y .. moron. Another interesting point about "Blacks don't need Affirmative Action Clarence" is, remember when he was called before the Senate hearings to answer charges of sexual harassment by Anita Hill? What was one of the first statements to come out of his mouth? That the hearings represented just another lynching of a Black man in America. Excuse me, but if he felt that racism was still alive and active, why wouldn't he feel that discrimination was still alive and active? And as a consequence, if those conditions still existed, would that not suggest a need for the continuation of some type of Affirmative Action program for minorities? Boys and girls, can you say hy .. po .. cri .. ti .. cal?

In order to succeed in this society you must be able to compete. Competition is about advantages versus disadvantages. In order to compete you must learn and understand the system in which you are competing. Now about this statement of "making it based on your own merit and ability." My friends, White folks know that this is only half of the game. You see, once you develop your skills and abilities, you must then develop a competitive edge or advantage—something to give you an edge over your competition; something to separate you from all of the other Business Administration majors, brick layers, comedians, etc., etc. Get the picture? Sometimes an edge is provided simply because of the school that you attended. Another edge could come from who you know and who knows you. Advantages can be provided in many ways and they can be developed in many ways. For example, I have always tried to work harder and learn different jobs once I was on the job in order to develop an edge over others in promotions and continued employment decisions. Another competitive edge, if the competition is between Blacks and Whites for available opportunities, is being White. Preferential treatment to Whites is a norm in this society that gives them a competitive edge over Blacks coming out of the starting gate. This is a major point of frustration for many Blacks. They feel let down because many do develop their skills and abilities, but the competitive advantages seem to always go to their White competitors. Affirmative Action has at least allowed them "the opportunity" to compete. White Americans for the most part are acutely aware of their advantages in open competition against Blacks for jobs, education, political, and economic opportunities. For Whites to say that everything is now equal is simply absurd. They know better. The only difference in the White Right of Heritage Affirmative Action plan and the Affirmative Action plan for minorities is that one is written and one is unwritten.

You want another example of White hypocrisy? Try this one on for size. I have a lot of Black friends who are administrators, directors, managers, supervisors, and consultants. They have shared with me that many of the White companies for which they work and their White employees have from time to time raised the issue, to them, that they feel like there are too many Blacks in high level positions within their particular areas or operations. They indicate that this situation creates a bad perception for the other employees. Ut Oh! We gotta do something; this is not right. Where was the concern when only Whites were allowed in those positions? Where are the concerns today, in many companies who still don't have any Blacks in so-called high positions? Oh! Incidentally, I have heard those comments also, I just didn't want to tell anybody, because I didn't think anybody would believe me. Who in their right mind would believe that White folks could fix their lips to make a statement like that?

Remember the Rodney King embarrassment? Remember how all of America tuned in to watch White policemen beat the pure dee hell out of an unarmed Black man who they claimed at first was on PCP? It was determined later that there were no PCP drugs in his system. Next they said that he had them fearful for their lives. This was, of course, as he lay on the ground broken, bleeding, and urinating on himself from the force of their unrelenting blows and electrical shocks. Remember how we were told by the White policemen, that IF he had not tried to escape, IF he had not been a criminal, and IF he would have just stayed on the ground, he would not have received the beating that he received. Remember the ALL White jury that found them innocent, as in their minds, the White policemen were JUST doing their jobs and JUST protecting themselves? Remember? This incident just served to support what Black Americans had been saying all along about how in many cases they were the victims of White police brutality. But their claims were always discounted. Even when the proof was there for all to see, the White jurors saw fit to exonerate the White policemen because after all the victim was a Black man with a criminal record, who probably had done something at sometime in his life to deserve the treatment that he got. The only reason the policemen were eventually tried and found guilty was because the Federal government stepped in, selected a mixed jury, and prosecuted them on Federal charges. Can we all just get along?

I bring up the King case because it represents a classic example of how preferential treatment can and does often work in a majority of White versus Black scenarios and why Black Americans are suspicious of the system. I also suspect that the real reason Blacks differed with Whites in their opinion as to whether O.J. Simpson was guilty or not had little to do with the fact that they actually thought he was innocent but rather with the results of the first King trial. When the issue was raised by the defense that there was a possibility that the police had framed O.J., many Blacks could readily relate to that possibility based on their own experiences or personal perceptions of how the system deals with Black folks on a daily and regular basis. They remembered what the system did to Rodney and they said to themselves, it could be possible. Whites on the other hand believed this was a ridiculous assumption because the facts were there for all to see. Blacks, however, remembered that the facts were there for all to see in the King beating, but it did not seem to matter. Justice was again reserved just for the White folks.

What I have tried to show in this book is how hypocritical some White folks and some of their status appointed Black clones are in their demands for an end to Affirmative Action. But, if you think that the purpose of this book is to provide excuses for Black American's societal failures, then you need to think again. Black Americans are no different than White Americans. They are people with desires, feelings, and the drives of basic human traits and needs. They have achieved under extremely adverse conditions and they will continue to achieve. They are no different than other groups who have experienced adversity. The problem is their legacy of torment and adversity is visible for all to see in the color of their skin. They cannot disguise or hide that color, they cannot easily assimilate into the masses and proclaim to be something other than they are. This makes them the perfect target for those who seek to identify differences in others as a basis for their own personal desire and need to be considered "better than."

Blacks have been the victims of power and control in America, but that does not make them "less than" or Whites "better than." It does not mean that White folks are evil and that Black folks are good. It simply means that Blacks are still in the process of establishing a legacy here in America. In order to establish that legacy, we have to develop a power base that will allow us as a group to successfully operate within this environment. We have to develop and maintain tools that will insure the continuance of that power base in order to establish a Black Right of Heritage. If we, as Black folks and a minority in this country, want to be treated equal, then we have to bring more to the table than fits of righteous indignation and condemnation concerning the way we are treated by the majority population. We have to establish a power base and use that base as leverage to demand equality, not just complain about inequality. We have the means and we have the power. We need to *just do it*. I hope Nike does not mind me borrowing that phrase.

There is a lot of attention and discussion concerning the negative state of race relations in this country today, which was one of the reasons that I wanted to write this book. The President is in the process of creating a commission to study ways to improve race relations and many cities and states have already created citizen commissions for the same purpose. The rise in racial hate crimes and the disingenuous efforts by the conservative right in America to eliminate Affirmative Action programs both seem to exacerbate the race relation problems between Blacks and Whites. Can we agree that the best way to improve race relations in this country is simply to treat people like we want to be treated. Next, can we agree that White folks, as a group, probably do receive preferential treatment in this system and that Blacks, as a group, probably don't? Finally, can we agree that human nature does play a major role in how we as people deal with each other, individually and as members of specific groups? If we can agree, then we can come to grips with the real problems. This will allow us to work together to resolve our problems. Sounds simple, doesn't it. It's not, but I believe that it will go a long way towards establishing trust between the two groups. The only way that we can improve race relations between White folks and Black folks is to create a climate in which both parties can trust each other. Today, that climate does not exist.

The next best way to improve race relations in this country is to read this book and encourage others to do likewise. I truly believe that I have provided some meaningful commentary as to why we have the problems that we do in Black on White interactions. I have tried to provide a basis for why the two groups view these problems from a different mind-set. I hope that those who read this book will understand that when you are talking about people, you cannot make a statement that will include ALL of any group. All Whites are not good people and all Blacks are not bad people. Black Americans would not have been freed from slavery without White involvement. Black Americans would not have been able to accomplish what they have in such a short period of time were it not for White assistance. So I don't want to hear that I said ALL White folks are this or ALL Black folks are that. But you have to judge a system based on how it impacts groupings as a whole, in order to get a true picture of how the system works.

Let me close by providing the following suggestions: If White folks would quit trying to convince Black folks that the system does not provide Whites with an advantage over Blacks because of their color, then we might be able to trust some of the other things that they say. This is not a colorblind society, but White folks want US to act like it is. They don't or can't, so how can we? Black folks need to admit that they, by some of THEIR actions, must share some of the blame for the creation of some of their problems. Black folks need to pretend that discrimination, racism, White preferential treatment to other Whites, and racial biases do not exist, with respect to allowing their existence to keep them from attaining an education or reaching their personal goals. However, Blacks need to understand that these conditions do exist in terms of providing them with an incentive to better develop their resources, personal abilities, and competitive edge.

If we start from those bases, we can resolve our problems. Because, after all, we all share the American Right of Heritage, the right to freedom, justice, and equality for all. However, you must remember, there is a significant difference between ideology and reality.

Thanks for reading. I hope you enjoyed. May God bless.

About the Author

The author was born and grew up in a northwest Arkansas community during the 1940s. He enjoyed the privileges of drinking from *Colored Only* water fountains, using *Colored Only* bathrooms, and attending a *Negro Only* elementary school and high school. He saw service in the United States Air Force during the Vietnam Conflict after being asked not to return to a majority group college in the mid 1960s for academic and disciplinary reasons.

He obtained a degree in Journalism from a majority group college after military service using GI Bill benefits. The author has work experiences as an administrator in city government, Personnel Generalist for government training programs, Representative for Social Services assistance programs, Instructor for civilian and military Race Relations seminars, and a Management Analyst for a major military training organization. He has accomplished graduate work in the fields of Human Resource management, Race and Human Relations studies, and Advanced Military Officer studies. He enjoys community affairs involvement and his role as a grandfather. The author wants you to read this book because after all, understanding is everything.